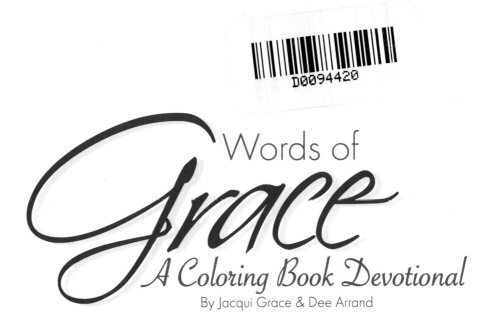

Words of *Grace*
A Coloring Book Devotional

By Jacqui Grace & Dee Arrand

BETHANYHOUSE

a division of Baker Publishing Group
Minneapolis, Minnesota

Illustrations © 2016 by Jacqui Grace
Text © 2016 by Dee Arrand

Published by Bethany House Publishers
11400 Hampshire Avenue South
Bloomington, Minnesota 55438
www.bethanyhouse.com

Bethany House Publishers is a division of
Baker Publishing Group, Grand Rapids, Michigan

Bethany House edition published 2017
ISBN 978-0-7642-3013-4

Previously published in the UK by Just Cards Publishing, a division of Just Cards Direct Limited.

Printed in the United States of America

17 18 19 20 21 22 23   7 6 5 4 3 2 1

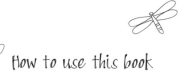

How to use this book

As with our coloring books, *Words of Grace* is designed to help you take
time out from the busyness of life and spend time with God. The images and
words are carefully woven together to provide a deeper understanding of Scripture,
so that as you color, you can prayerfully consider their meaning for your life.

This devotional offers a great resource for both groups and individuals. Structured over 28
days, the devotions are based on Scripture verses, centered on different aspects of God's
grace. The four parts of the book can be completed consecutively, or as topical studies. Each
devotion flows into a time of coloring, prayer, and reflection.

Use in a group
The book is suitable for Bible study groups, creative groups, or prayer groups.

At the end of each week, you will find four reflective questions, which can be used to help a
group discuss the theme of the week and unpack the journey through the book. Alternatively,
groups might like to chat through their completed coloring pages, sharing how God may have
spoken to them during the process.

Use by individuals
As you color, think through the words of the devotion alongside the image. Allow
God to minister to you as you do.

This is your book and hopefully a precious part of your journey
with God. Personalize it! You might like to add notes or
your own continuation of a drawing to enhance
the picture.

Foreword

Words of Grace is a wonderful combination of daily devotions and accompanying illustrations.

Building on the success of Jacqui Grace's inspirational first coloring book, *Images of Grace*, Jacqui has added eight new designs and enhanced several others, to create a perfect accompaniment for these thoughts.

I am delighted that Dee Arrand has written the devotions. She brings with her many years of experience of helping countless individuals to find emotional and spiritual healing through a living God. She has sensitively and creatively penned the reflections, producing a unique marriage of words and art. The illustrations can be colored or simply used as inspiration for prayer.

Grace is a fantastic theme for these daily thoughts and I pray that this month of dwelling on God's word will be both awe-inspiring and life-changing for everyone who turns these pages.

Anne Horrobin
Director, Just Cards Publishing

The Authors

"It's been exciting to hear stories and testimonies of how the coloring books, *Images of Grace* and *Images of Hope*, have enabled people to spend creative time with God, meditating on His word.

Following on from this, I have been delighted and honored to have been part of this new adventure, working together with Dee to take this concept a step further. Dee's inspired words help unpack the Scripture verses at a deeper level.

My hope is that as you carve out time to be with God, and put the busyness of life on hold, He will meet with you in a fresh and powerful way. I pray that as you color and meditate, you will be receptive as God speaks to you and His truth will sink deeply into your heart and mind."

Jacqui Grace

"What a privilege to be involved in producing a devotional designed for the creatively inclined!

Thinking and praying through the Scriptures, alongside Jacqui's beautiful images, has been an amazing privilege for me. My hope is that these devotions bring together both the truth of God's word and the deep reality of His limitless love and grace.

My prayer is that as you work through this book, you will not only find refreshment and encouragement, but life-changing encounters with our Creator and Savior."

Dee Arrand

God's Awesome Love

"This is love, not that we loved God, but that He loved us and sent His Son" (1 John 4:10)

Some verses in the Bible can leave us feeling completely overwhelmed by the graciousness of God, and this is one of them! It seems beyond human comprehension that He should lavish this kind of undeserved favor on sinful people.

For many of us, becoming a Christian isn't a "black then white" moment of dramatic transformation. It is a gradual journey to the point of realizing our need of a Savior and inviting Jesus into our lives. The relentless grace of God draws us to Him, and His irresistible love keeps us growing in our faith.

Why would a holy and pure God want anything to do with us, with all our insecurities and failings—and even before we ever loved Him? His glorious grace is far beyond any human love we can imagine. His astonishing love for us, even when we disobey Him, is sometimes termed "outrageous." It is perhaps best described in John 3:16:

"For God so loved the world that He gave His only begotten Son, that whoever believes in Him should not perish but have everlasting life."

The Lord wants us to spend eternity with Him—what a privilege!

We are saved the moment we agree with God that we are not righteous or faultless, confess our sins, and accept Jesus Christ, His Son, as our Savior and the Lord of our lives. This is the beginning of our walk as children of God.

Not only does our merciful God not give us what we do deserve (punishment for our sins), but He also gives us what we don't deserve—His grace and favor, both in saving us and in all His everyday dealings with us. Through Christ's life, death, and resurrection, we can *"come boldly to the throne of grace, that we may obtain mercy and find grace to help in time of need"* (Hebrews 4:16).

You may like to praise God for the wonderful rescue plan He has designed for us, or to ponder the awesomeness of His love. What a Savior!

1 John 4 · verse 10

In this is love, not that we loved God, but that He loved us and sent His Son

DAY 02

Set Apart for God

"He chose us in Him before the foundation of the world" (Ephesians 1:4)

There is something very affirming and heartwarming about moments when we are noticed and chosen. As children, being chosen last for a sports team or activity may have been one of the things we feared most. Being rejected often makes us feel embarrassed, empty, and worthless. We all want to feel chosen—rejection hurts.

As God's children, we need never fear rejection by Him. Ephesians 1:4 assures us that He thinks so much of us that He chose us before the foundation of the world. He has had us in mind for a long time!

This verse reassures us of our significance to God. It reminds us that He has plans and purposes for our lives, and they are not some random outworking of fate. His hand is upon us, and He desires for us to have an intimate relationship with Him every day.

It can be a wonderful feeling to be chosen or included in any situation. Just think—God Himself, the Almighty Creator of Heaven and earth, set you apart for a life with Him. This life in relationship with God is not always easy, but allowing the Holy Spirit to transform us to be more like Him, is wonderfully exciting, as well as challenging.

As we have been chosen and loved, so we are called to love one another (John 13:34-35). This may sound simple, but we all know that it can be a struggle at times. Loving those who we perceive as difficult, or those who have hurt us, needs to be done humbly and intentionally, in God's strength.

As you color, allow God to minister His affection to you. What is your response?

Are there people who you find tough to love? Maybe there might be someone that you need to forgive today?

Ask God to give you a love for everyone in your life, especially those you find difficult.

Belonging to God

"Thus says the LORD, he who created you, O Jacob, he who formed you, O Israel: 'Fear not, for I have redeemed you; I have called you by name, you are mine'" (Isaiah 43:1, ESV)

If we struggle with any kind of fear in our lives, this verse is a significant encouragement.

God, the Lord of Lords, created us and says that we are His!

When we become parents or "birth" something (such as an idea that comes to fruition), we have a great personal interest and sense of pride that keeps us connected and wanting to nurture, nourish, and protect that creation. If we feel this way about our children or something close to our hearts, how much more does God care about us—His unique creation whom He knit together in our mother's womb (Psalm 139:13, ESV)?

We are also told not to fear in this verse because the Lord has redeemed us. *Redeemed* is not a word that we use very much in everyday conversation! One definition is "to gain or regain possession of (something) in exchange for payment." Why should God need to buy us back? As sinful people, we have all fallen from grace and lived without God, according to our own desires.

God's plan is to "buy us back" through Jesus Christ, who left His place in glory with the Father and lived on earth as the Son of Man. He died on the Cross as a perfect sacrifice for the sins of the world and was raised to life through the power of God. Whoever has given their heart to Jesus, and made Him their Lord, has eternal life!

This verse finally urges us not to fear because God has called us by our names. Names are essential to our identity and have much meaning and significance. For the Lord to say He has called you by your name is a very intimate statement. What is more, He knows not only your name but also exactly how many hairs there are on your head (Matthew 10:30)! He cares about the smallest details of our lives.

With these amazing encouragements in mind, we should "fear not," whatever happens to us in life, for we have been created by God, redeemed, and called by name. What a privilege!

Isaiah 43:1
(ESV)

fear NOT FOR I Have Called YOU BY NAME You are MINE

Relying on Christ

"For by grace you have been saved through faith. And this is not your own doing; it is the gift of God" (Ephesians 2:8, ESV)

DAY 04

Jesus Christ, the only Son of the Father, became flesh and lived as a man so that through Him the work of grace would bring salvation, the saving power of God for all people.

Our Christian life is not about what we can do or how well we perform, but rather about acknowledging our need for a Savior and trusting that God will use us to fulfill His purposes.

The Law that was given through Moses provided a template for living in right relationship with God, other people, and the world around us. The need for this extensive set of rules demonstrates that, as human beings, we don't tend to get it right all the time—we sin all too easily. No one has to teach a child to do wrong!

As humans we cannot trust in our own goodness to achieve a right relationship with God.

Through faith, we must rely on the immeasurable grace and mercy of God to help us. If we could receive God's favor through our own effort and determination, Christ would not have needed to die for us.

This does not mean, however, that we should not bother trying to live righteously. Some people believe that because we are under grace, we can live however we like. This makes a mockery of the Cross and the amazing sacrifice of Jesus on our behalf. If we respond to this sacrifice in a loving, thankful way, we will seek to follow God's purposes for our lives.

All God requires of us is to have faith in Him, and we cannot even produce this ourselves—He gives it to us as a free gift! Faith is about trusting God and getting out of the boat as Jesus beckons us to walk with Him on the waters of life, however stormy they may be.

for by GRACE you have been SAVED through faith

Ephesians 2 v 8

Crowned by the King

"Bless the LORD, O my soul . . . who redeems your life from the pit, who crowns you with steadfast love and mercy" (Psalm 103:1,4 ESV)

"Crown Him with many crowns, the Lamb upon His throne;
Hark how the heavenly anthem drowns all music but its own!
Awake, my soul, and sing of Him who died for thee,
And hail Him as thy matchless King through all eternity."[1]

The words of this beautiful hymn paint a marvelous picture of the Lord in His glory. Each verse praises a different aspect of God's character, with lines beginning "Crown Him the Lord of life," "the Lord of love," "the Lord of peace," and "the Lord of years." It echoes the picture of majesty created in Psalm 103:19 (ESV), which says: *"The LORD has established his throne in the heavens, and his kingdom rules over all."*

Amazingly, as today's verse from Psalm 103:4 shows, God reflects this glory and honor back on us. **He crowns us with steadfast love and mercy.**

A crown being placed on the head has great ceremonial significance. In the United Kingdom, Queen Elizabeth II was empowered as monarch through a series of profoundly important events, one of which was the setting of a jeweled crown on her head as a symbol of her new sovereignty.

The King of Kings and Lord of Lords has placed upon His children's heads the most amazing crown. This crown is one not made of earthly materials like diamonds or gemstones, which although precious, have no eternal value. Instead, He crowns us with steadfast love and mercy that will remain with us forever!

This honor is not something we can earn or to which we have any right. It is through the immense favor and astonishing grace of God that we are given this crown to wear.

How can the knowledge that you are wearing this crown make a difference in your life? Remember that this makes us royal children—not the ruling family of a single country, but sons and daughters of the King of the universe. What an encouragement for times when we might feel rejected or discouraged!

[1] Bridges, Matthew. *"Crown Him with Many Crowns".* Published in many hymnals; originally published 1851.

Psalm 103:4

HE crowns you with steadfast LOVE and MERCY

Belonging to the Flock

"Make a joyful shout to the LORD, all you lands! Serve the LORD with gladness; Come before His presence with singing. Know that the LORD, He is God; It is He who has made us, and not we ourselves; We are His people and the sheep of His pasture" (Psalm 100:1-3)

Psalm 100 is a wonderful call to praise!

The invitation to *"make a joyful shout to the Lord"* is made to all of us, whether musically gifted or not. This picture of each of God's people contributing something unique and special to the collective "song," expresses the importance of belonging to His family.

And the reason we are called to praise the Lord?

He is God and we are His! He has created us and lovingly cares for us as a shepherd does his flock.

We each have a God-given desire to belong, not only to Him but to each other. So why do we humans also love independence and strive for self-sufficiency? Of course, using our initiative and being resourceful are positive traits. But, if we are honest, perhaps sometimes our pride and sense of self-importance drive us to show the world that we can "go it alone." If we have been hurt or offended by others, we may try to defend ourselves by withdrawing and creating barriers in our relationships. Sadly, pulling away from God or others can leave us feeling miserable and alone.

In Matthew 22:37-39, we are reminded that our true purpose is to love God and others: *"Jesus said to him, 'You shall love the LORD your God with all your heart, with all your soul, and with all your mind.' This is the first and great commandment. And the second is like it: 'You shall love your neighbor as yourself.'"*

The description in Psalm 100:3 of Christians being "the sheep of His pasture" also shows that we were made for relationship both with God and others. Sheep thrive in flocks, not alone. We need each other and can all contribute in various unique ways in the churches and communities in which we live.

Are you connected to the flock? If not, why not look for a local church that you could join?

If you are connected, how might you build up others in the body of Christ in a new way?

How Do You See Yourself?

"The LORD is gracious and merciful, slow to anger and abounding in steadfast love"
(Psalm 145:8, ESV)

This psalm is brimming with the assurance of the Lord's overwhelming compassion. His love is an anchor for our souls. He looks at us with grace and mercy, patience, and kindness.

Think for a moment about how you view yourself—do you value and treasure the fact that you are made in God's image, the work of His hands? Do you view yourself with kindness and grace or do you sometimes dislike or even hate yourself?

We all respond to how we were first treated as babies and through our impressionable childhood years. If we were loved, affirmed, and encouraged we are likely to have a positive attitude toward ourselves and feel confident that God loves us too. If our early years had a negative influence, we may question our worth and potential. Our Creator wants to help us change any negative cycles, where we treat ourselves badly, and bring us to a point of accepting and loving both ourselves and others.

As we allow the truth of the Lord's mercy and acceptance to permeate our hearts, we can start treating ourselves with the same grace and love that God shows us. In Luke 6:36 (ESV) we are encouraged to *"Be merciful, even as your Father is merciful."* Perhaps this applies to not just how we treat others, but ourselves as well?

If you struggle with a negative self-image, use God's word to look up verses that affirm the truth about your worth and value. You could put these verses on your fridge, commit them to memory or study them in depth with a friend. As you color today, ask Jesus to speak His truth about yourself into your spirit.

Group Questions:

1. As you have journeyed through this first week of devotions, what has impacted you the most?

2. Read Ephesians 2:4–9. It says that we have been saved by grace through faith, not by works. What encourages you and challenges you about this passage?

3. Do you have a salvation story of your own? Would you like to share it with the group?

4. In groups of 2–3, honestly share how you see yourself. Pray and listen to Jesus for how he views you and each other.

Blessed Refreshment

"Come to Me, all you who labor and are heavy laden, and I will give you rest"
(Matthew 11:28)

Being "at rest" will mean varying things to different people and can evoke a number of images. Sometimes we have a wrong understanding of rest that can sabotage our ability to embrace it in our lives. For some, it may feel like being lazy, or even be seen as wasting time.

At the start of history, the curtains opened on a magnificent stage on which God made everything good that has ever been made, including mankind, out of nothing! Then, on the seventh day, what did God do?

Genesis 2:2-3 (ESV) says: *"And on the seventh day God finished his work that he had done, and he rested on the seventh day from all his work that he had done. So God blessed the seventh day and made it holy, because on it God rested from all his work that he had done in creation."* **This set a precedent for mankind and it formed a life-pattern that is meant to bless, sustain, and refresh us.**

This fundamental principle of working for six days and resting on one day is seen repeated across the pages of the Bible, including in the instruction to allow land to lie fallow every seventh year. This idea of Sabbath rest is so fundamental to life that the Lord includes it in the Ten Commandments (Exodus 20:8-11).

As God's people traveled on their epic Exodus journey toward the Promised Land, He said: *"My Presence will go with you, and I will give you rest"* (Exodus 33:14). There is something about the Presence of God that can give us a profound sense of peace. Being with the Lord and serving Him is not about striving, but about allowing our lives to center on Him and letting Him do His work through us. We all want to avoid stress and burnout, so it is important that we carry only what the Lord wants us to be responsible for and prayerfully lay down what is left.

What does this place of rest mean for you?
Perhaps consider whether it holds enough importance in your life.

Growing in God's Vineyard

"As the Father has loved me, so have I loved you. Abide in my love." (John 15:9, ESV)
You may find it helpful to read John 15:1-17 before beginning this devotion.

DAY 09

When Jesus walked the earth, He traveled through the countryside around Jerusalem and the surrounding towns and villages. The hot Mediterranean sun, the scent of wayside flowers, and the sight of local crops, animals, and people gave Him great scope for telling parables to those who followed Him. He vividly illustrated truths about God's Kingdom, using scenes from everyday life and the culture around Him. These include references to vines and their cultivation, which He speaks of in John 15.

He begins by explaining that He is the true vine (v.1), and we are the branches, born to bear productive harvests of fruit (v.5). He describes how pruning will produce the best fruit (v.2) and how we cannot live a productive life without Him (v.5). When we live with Jesus at the center of our existence, there are no limits to what we can achieve through Him, as verse 7 says: *"If you abide in me, and my words abide in you, ask whatever you wish, and it will be done for you"* (ESV). Now that's exciting!

The Lord's invitation to us is to "abide in Him." to live and remain so close to Him that everything we do will flow out from this loving relationship.

We often cheerfully go to great lengths to be with the one we love and spend as much time with them as possible. When we are separated from them we can feel empty, and long for a quick reunion. In the same way, as we receive more revelation about how much God loves us, our hearts respond with a desire to spend more time with Him. Of course, the ultimate reunion will take place when Jesus returns for His Bride, the Church, and we are able to spend eternity with Him, the "lover of our souls."

As you go through today, consider how you might abide in His love.

ABIDE IN MY LOVE

John 15 v 9

Intimacy with the Father

"The Mighty One will save. . . . He will quiet you with His love, He will rejoice over you with singing" (Zephaniah 3:17)

This Scripture is like a big, warm, all-embracing hug!

It shows the tenderness, compassion, intimacy, and security of God's deep love for us. It lays the foundation for our safety in His everlasting arms (Deuteronomy 33:27).

The verse describes our Creator God, our Defender and the One who loves us so much that He sent His only beloved Son, Jesus Christ. He came to earth as a man, to die for our sins on the Cross, and to be raised to life so that we could have eternal life in Him. He is the One who saves us! He wants the best for us and for our future—both on this earth, and in eternity with Him.

He will *"quiet us with His love."* In today's culture, there is so much noise. It is often difficult to find a still, silent, or set-aside place to simply **be**. But wherever we are—either in our own private space or, possibly, away at a place of retreat, God offers to meet with us and give us that longed-for stillness and rest.

Psalm 23 paints a stunningly beautiful picture of Jesus, our Good Shepherd, walking with us along a path beside still waters. However, this passage in Zephaniah describes an even more intimate place of peace and safety, wrapped in His tender arms of love. It is a place so close to Him that we can hear the special, unique song that He sings over each one of us!

Can you hear Him rejoicing over you today? Take time to draw near to God because, if we do, He has promised to draw near to us (James 4:8). Try to spend some time today in a quiet place, listening to Father God. What is He saying to you and how might you respond?

DAY 11

Trusting in God

"Trust in the LORD, and do good; dwell in the land, and feed on His faithfulness. Delight yourself also in the LORD, and He shall give you the desires of your heart. . . . Rest in the LORD, and wait patiently for Him" (Psalm 37:3–4, 7)

Trust develops through the gradual building of a relationship. We learn to trust the Lord more and more as we get to know Him better. We discover that He is faithful, true, and dependable.

Trust is about *resting* in God and not striving to make things happen by ourselves. Every good parent wants to cherish, protect, and provide for their children; God, who is the perfect Father, wants to do the same for us. He longs for His children to rely on Him, not on ourselves, and to live in a place of security and joy, whatever our circumstances might be. How many of us long for that in these days of uncertainty?

This Scripture speaks about *"delighting in the Lord."* What does this mean for you? There are many ways in which we can delight in Him, especially by putting Him first and by choosing to love and serve Him in all circumstances. As we allow Him to be central in our lives, He will give us the desires of our hearts—desires that He probably planted there in the first place!

Verse 7 says: *"Rest in the Lord, and wait patiently for Him."* The waiting is not easy! We live in a microwave kind of world, where we want everything now. Sometimes God seems more like a slow cooker . . . but His timing is always *perfect*! Patiently waiting for Him to act allows us to develop a childlike trust in our Heavenly Father.

Have a look at the picture alongside this Scripture: you will see there are seeds planted in deep places. These may represent dreams or visions cherished deep in our hearts. You may have the seeds of ideas, or half-grown sprouting shoots, or a full-blown, fruitful, mature 'living-it-now' dream! Spend some time coloring, and, as you do, allow the Lord to show you what He has planted in your life—what is even now growing and reaching fulfillment. His will is to bless you and give you a personal calling that cannot be taken away. As Romans 11:29 says, *"the gifts and the calling of God are irrevocable."* Now that's grace!

Let us, like the psalmist, rest in the Lord and wait patiently for Him to act. He will do what He has promised, as we trust in Him.

Amazed by Grace

"Grow in the grace and knowledge of our Lord and Saviour Jesus Christ" (2 Peter 3:18)

Grace, according to Oxford Dictionaries, is the "free and unmerited favor of God."

"Amazing Grace"[1] by John Newton is one of the most famous and beautiful hymns of all time. Its words, including the opening line *"Amazing grace! How sweet the sound that saved a wretch like me!"* and *"'tis grace that brought me safe thus far, and grace will lead me home,"* leave one in no doubt of the power and marvel of God's grace.

2 Corinthians 12:9 says, *"My grace is sufficient for you, for My strength is made perfect in weakness."* God's grace is indeed sufficient for us, particularly when we rely on it completely. As long as we feel that we can manage by relying on our own strength and resources, we may struggle to experience the fullness of God's presence and power.

It is a hard moment when we realize that we have run out of our own, or man's, solutions, but it can also be the most thrilling. For when the Lord is the only One we rely on, we discover that He is literally more than enough! This is when we see miracles. This is when we experience the power of God in our everyday lives.

Through this process of surrender, humility, and trust in God, we find the space to develop our lives with Him. As we grow in acceptance of this amazing grace, our relationship with our Savior and Lord will also increase.

Every one of us can likely testify to some measure of grace in our lives. As you color, think about the times when God's grace has broken through into your life, and perhaps offer praise to Jesus for these experiences.

Are you going through a situation right now that seems impossible in human terms?

You might like to ask the Lord for His grace and power to bring you through.

[1] Newton, John. "Amazing Grace". Published in many hymnals; first published 1779.

GROW IN Grace

"...grow in the grace and knowledge of our Lord and savior Jesus Christ"

2 Peter 3v 18

Drawing Near to God

"Draw near to God, and he will draw near to you" (James 4:8, ESV)

DAY 13

This verse is an invitation for us to enter into a deeper relationship with our Creator God! Imagine Him holding out His hands toward you with loving eyes, saying "Come close; let's enjoy one another's company." This is not a passive gesture, but a longing on His part for deeper friendship and intimacy. If we don't want to accept His invitation, He will not force us, but like the father in the Parable of the Lost Son (Luke 15:11–31), He will come running out to meet us when we make the first move toward Him.

Drawing near to God is not about drifting aimlessly toward Him, but rather more of a deliberate decision to seek Him and include Him in our day-to-day lives. When we do that, He promises, in turn, to draw near to us and our relationship with Him will grow and flourish. We are never equal with God, yet He longs to walk with us and talk with us along the journey of life.

So where do you best meet with God? Creating a regular time and place to meet with your Savior and Friend allows Him to challenge, encourage, and refresh you. You might like to take long walks alone in the countryside, where nature reflects His presence, listen to music, work in the garden, put a brush to canvas, or just sit quietly, allowing God's word to speak to your heart. Wherever it is, it is a chance to connect with God and listen to Him, without the many distractions of home or work.

For some of us, working in the garden can give us a profound revelation of His heart and character. Removing weeds and stones, digging over the soil and finally planting the precious seed, are processes that speak to us about the ways in which God, as the Divine Gardener, works in our lives to produce fruitfulness.

Where do you best hear and meet with the Lord?

Try and make time this week to spend quality time with Him in that special place.

Finding Rest in Him

"Be still, and know that I am God" (Psalm 46:10)

DAY 14

It can sometimes be difficult to step aside and find a quiet moment of stillness in the hustle and bustle of our busy, demanding lives.

Often, our daily routines show that we are less human beings and more humans doing! This passage is a personal invitation from God Himself—He longs for us to shift our gaze from the details of our own lives and look *"unto Jesus, the author and finisher of our faith"* (Hebrews 12:2). Time spent in stillness with God draws us closer to Him and refocuses us on who He is and His purpose for our lives.

The Lord's Prayer (Matthew 6:9-13) includes the words, *"Your kingdom come, Your will be done."* But sometimes we become so busy, distracted and caught up in our own activity that we are really building our own "kingdoms" and letting our own desires rule.

The purpose of seeking stillness is to know God more. In a quiet place, we can learn to hear His voice over our own and those of the world. Submerging ourselves in the Word and prayer opens the way for God to speak and lead. We can begin to understand His passion and desire for our lives, so that our priorities are in line with, not working against, our loving Creator God.

As we take a break to spend time with God, it may help to remind ourselves exactly who He is. The following attributes may help you to focus on His character:

- He is the Prince of Peace (Isaiah 9:6)
- He is All-powerful (Jeremiah 32:17)
- He is Sovereign (Daniel 4:35)
- He is Holy (1 Peter 1:14-16)
- He is Righteous (Psalm 145:17)

Before you start to color, perhaps spend some time with the Lord—not requesting anything from Him, but simply giving Him praise for who He is, and then remaining still in His love.

Group Questions:

1. This week we have been challenged to rest in God and find a place of intimacy with Him. How do you feel about this challenge and why?

2. Read John 15:1-11. What 3 things challenge you about this passage?

3. What is the best time, place, and setting for you to meet with God? Share ideas with the group.

4. In groups of 2-3, share the dreams and visions that you have for your life. Pray into them together.

BE Still AND kNOW THAT I AM GOD

Psalm 46 verse 10.

DAY 15

Abundant Life

"I have come that they may have life, and that they may have it more abundantly"
(John 10:10)

The word *life* is synonymous with hope, fullness of joy, abundance, and new beginnings. It calls to mind the promise and expectation of springtime, when green shoots burst forth following the chill of winter.

Life is the opposite of death—not only of the body, but also of our hopes and dreams. It can feel gut-wrenchingly painful when our dreams come crashing down around us. Our sense of failure or disappointment can be overwhelming, draining our strength and joy.

Most of us would love to bounce out of bed each day with endless energy and joy, but sustaining that throughout life is not often possible. We all naturally experience troughs as well as peaks. Challenging life events or illness may slow us down and steal our joy and, for some, life can become increasingly frustrating as our bodies age and we aren't able to do as much as we once could.

So when Jesus Himself offers us abundant life, what does it look like? He says in John 14:6: *"I am the way, the truth, and the life,"* and in John 11:25: *"I am the resurrection and the life."* He also reassures us that it is

"in Him [that] we live and move and have our being" (Acts 17:28). When we live in Jesus, our experience of life is guided by our relationship with Him, not just by our circumstances.

Despite how we may feel at a natural level, God wants to reassure us with His peace and joy, that will last not just through our lives on earth, but on into the promised eternal life with Him.

Maybe you are feeling low and lacking in joy and energy today. Jesus is reaching out His hand to you, offering His help, life, and strength. **Sometimes the lowest points of our lives can become springboards that lead to fresh hope and a new chapter in life.**

As you color, consider making your reflections a prayer to God, accepting the abundant life He offers. Perhaps He has also laid on your heart someone else to pray for, who may be in particular need of His strength and renewal today.

JESUS SAID..."I AM THE WAY, AND THE TRUTH, AND THE LIFE. NO ONE COMES TO THE FATHER EXCEPT THROUGH ME." JOHN 14:6 (ESV)

Hope in the Darkness

"O LORD, You brought my soul up from the grave;
You have kept me alive,
that I should not go down to the pit" (v.3)
"Weeping may endure for a night,
But joy comes in the morning" (v.5)

"You have turned for me
my mourning into dancing;

You have put off my sackcloth and
clothed me with gladness,
To the end that my glory may
sing praise to You and not be silent.
O LORD my God,
I will give thanks to You forever" (v.11-12)
(Psalm 30)

Have you ever felt that the burden of grief you carry is so unbearable that it might consume you, pulling you under like a vast Atlantic breaker? Be assured today that you are not alone. The Lord cares deeply about your well-being.

When we are feeling low or suffering in some way, nighttimes can be especially hard. The walls seem to close in, and problems weigh on us more heavily. What a relief when that first streak of light appears on the horizon!

Psalm 30 is a powerful account of hope and thanksgiving in the midst of heart-wrenching emotional (and perhaps physical) pain. In this passage, David is not afraid to be real about exactly how he feels—from the dreadful blackness of *"the pit"* to the massive relief of deliverance by God, who *"turned my mourning into dancing."* Similar words are found in Isaiah and quoted by Jesus in the synagogue

(Luke 4:17-21). The prophet writes that God would send Jesus *'to comfort all who mourn . . . to give them beauty for ashes, the oil of joy for mourning, the garment of praise for the spirit of heaviness"* (Isaiah 61:2-3).

It is amazing how God gives us strategies to help us survive in our tough world. The shedding of tears, for example, can help to bring relief as we pour out our woe and anxiety. David continually cries out to God from the depths in this way. Despite the fear and torment he is obviously experiencing, he looks up from his circumstances and keeps returning to the fact that God is good, compassionate, faithful, and able to rescue him.

If you find yourself going through a difficult time right now, look to Him, the God of all comfort, for His reassurance and peace.

Certain as the Dawn

D A Y 1 7

"The steadfast love of the LORD never ceases; his mercies never come to an end; they are new every morning; great is your faithfulness" (Lamentations 3:22-23, ESV)

There is something uplifting about the start of a new day that can give us a sense of hope and optimism. It is like pressing the 'reset' button and starting afresh.

This Scripture describes God's mercy as being new every morning, never ending, and going on forever and ever. God is saying that each day, if we confess our sins and are walking with Him, that He presses the "reset" button in our lives, turning our status once more to "forgiven."

God is love—the boundless, steadfast love so beautifully described in 1 Corinthians 13. In His love, He removes our transgressions from us *"as far as the east is from the west"* (Psalm 103:12, ESV).

The Lord longs for us to walk in the hope and freedom that His love and forgiveness bring.

It is for this reason that He sent Jesus Christ, of whom He said *"This is my beloved Son, with whom I am well pleased"* (Matthew 3:17, ESV), to die on the Cross and take our sin, shame, and guilt upon Himself. 1 John 1:9 promises that *"if we confess our sins, he is faithful and just to forgive us our sins and to cleanse us from all unrighteousness"* (ESV). There are no exceptions, as no sin is too bad, and there are no conditions, except our confession and repentance.

This faithful, extraordinary, lavish love of God is available to all of us, afresh at the start of every new day, and throughout our lives.

As you color this picture, think about how God sees you. **Are you able to receive the truth that you are forgiven and loved?**

In Our Weakness

"But he said to me, 'My grace is sufficient for you, for my power is made perfect in weakness.' Therefore I will boast all the more gladly of my weaknesses, so that the power of Christ may rest upon me" (2 Corinthians 12:9, ESV)

How we love to feel strong and able and to have everything sorted in our lives! There may be times when we feel this way, but there will also be days, weeks, months, or even years when we feel weak or unable to cope with life's circumstances.

Does God abandon us in those moments? Of course not! When we are really struggling, we may think that God is waiting for us to get back on our feet or pull ourselves together. Maybe we imagine that He doesn't want anything to do with us when it's all gone wrong. This could not be further from the truth.

Scripture promises that it is precisely at these times of desperation that the Lord is willing and able to step into our lives, meet us where we are at, and carry us through the storm. He will *"supply every need of yours according to his riches in glory in Christ Jesus"* (Philippians 4:19, ESV).

As this passage in 2 Corinthians 12 suggests, when life is hard, we tend to lean on God's strength and provision; but when we have all we think we need, it is easy to ignore His life-giving power in our lives. **It is often during times of weakness that our faith is refined and strengthened, as the Lord's power and compassion is revealed.** With hindsight, it is easier to see how God carried us and worked to bring good from our struggles. Sometimes, our experiences prepare us to be used by God to minister to someone else in the future.

Are you in need of God's incomparable rescue today? Ask Him for faith to trust Him at this time. As we trust Him, we are strengthened and able to put one foot in front of the other in life and journey toward God's best for us.

2 CORINTHIANS 12:9.

MY grace is sufficient

Grace for Today

"This is the day that the LORD has made; let us rejoice and be glad in it" (Psalm 118:24, ESV)

How often do we stop and offer praise to God for each day, with all the ordinary and extraordinary things that happen? Psalm 118 challenges us to begin our days with thanksgiving for His mercy, power, and love. We miss out on so much when we live with too much focus on the past or future and do not take notice of what God is doing today.

Hebrews 13:8 tells us that, *"Jesus Christ is the same yesterday, today, and forever."* Remembering what God has done, and what He has promised to do, helps to give us a solid foundation for our faith. However, the Lord wants to communicate with us in every "now" moment too. So many times in Scripture, God says "I AM," telling us that He is relevant, active, and present.

When we live in the past, we may rely on experiences from years ago, including amazing encounters with God, rather than focusing on His provision in our present circumstances. We may also allow past hurt or regret to rule our lives, impacting the way we build relationships in the future.

*Yesterday is history;
Tomorrow is a mystery;
Today is a gift, which is why it is called "THE PRESENT!"*
-Anonymous

Isn't it also so easy to procrastinate—to put off till tomorrow what we should have done today? **When we fixate on the future, with all its possibilities, we miss out on "now" moments of grace.** We may even be in danger of putting off fully surrendering our hearts to Jesus, thinking "I'll do it tomorrow" but we just don't know whether tomorrow will come. Let us instead rejoice and be glad for every day that the Lord gives us, making the most of every opportunity!

The Bible urges us not to worry about the future, because He cares for us (Matthew 6:34). Let God take your burdens today, as He has promised to do. Rest in the knowledge that He is victorious—the Alpha and Omega, the Beginning and the End.

This is the day that the Lord has made; let us rejoice and be glad in it.

Psalm 118:24 (ESV)

Strong in Christ

"I can do all things through Christ who strengthens me" (Philippians 4:13)

The Bible tells us we can do all things through Christ. What a promise and an encouragement! We can learn to be overcomers, not on our own but through the grace and power of the Lord. This takes the pressure off us, doesn't it?

When we are weak and call out to God, His strength is revealed as the Holy Spirit empowers us. As 2 Corinthians 4:7 describes it, our bodies are like earthen vessels (or jars of clay) that hold an amazing treasure. That treasure is the Holy Spirit, who lives within each of God's children and is so powerful. We are told, in 1 John 4:4, that He *"is greater than he who is in the world [the Enemy]."* When we genuinely seek to do God's will, and *"seek first the kingdom of God and His righteousness"* (Matthew 6:33), we can rely on the power of God to enable us.

As Romans 8:11 explains, *"If the Spirit of Him who raised Jesus from the dead dwells in you, He who raised Christ from the dead will also give life to your mortal bodies through His Spirit who dwells in you."* God is able to give us life itself through the Holy Spirit and we can certainly trust Him to give us the strength to face all of life's challenges.

Many times in our lives, we wholeheartedly want to do what we believe the Lord is asking of us but cannot do it on our own. Each time, we need to rely on His provision for the task and journey. Sometimes we receive supernatural courage or faith, and other times, determination and resolve to bring us through. Either way, it is God who equips us!

Have there been times in your life when Christ gave you extra strength and ability to tackle a problem? Perhaps spend a few moments thanking Him, and think about how you can encourage others with stories of how God's power has been at work in your everyday circumstances.

Do you need God's strength in your life right now? He knows. He wants to draw near to you and fill you afresh with the life-giving, enabling Holy Spirit. Bring your situation before Him today.

DAY 21

Perfect Peace

"May grace and peace be yours in full measure!" (1 Peter 1:2, NET)

Generosity is a wonderful quality in anyone, but God is the ultimate generous giver! This Scripture was written from Peter to the scattered believers, but it also reflects God's heart for us.

Again and again, Scripture reassures us that God longs to pour into our lives everything of the bounty of Heaven. He is not a God who watches us from afar but, instead He gets involved with the minute details of our lives.

When stirred, He can also be a God of avenging wrath against injustice and lawlessness. Yet even in those intense times, He wants people to return to Him and receive His mercy. We read of His tenderness, likened in Matthew 23:37 to that of a mother hen with her chicks.

Peace is something that our hearts crave—that place of rest and security where fear has no place and our thoughts are still. Jesus Himself is the Prince of Peace (Isaiah 9:6), and the peace He gives us does not depend upon the circumstances around us. It is not worldly peace based on fragile material goods, or our physical safety, but a peace that is absolute and immovable (John 14:27).

How does the knowledge that God wants to bless us affect how you approach Him in prayer? You can bring your needs and desires before Him today, confident in His longing to give you grace and peace.

Group Questions:

1. We have talked a little about tough times this week. What has impacted you from the week's devotions and why?

2. Read Lamentations 3:19-26. Which verse jumps out to you and why?

3. Share a story from your life when you've struggled, felt desperate or weak. Looking back, how did God strengthen you and maybe even bring good out of the situation?

4. In groups of 2-3, share any current difficulties and pray for each other.

may Grace and peace be YOURS in FULL measure

1 Peter 1:2 NET

DAY 22

A Gift Like No Other

"Thanks be to God for his inexpressible gift" (2 Corinthians 9:15, ESV)

The idea of receiving a present fills most of us with excited anticipation. We realize that someone who knows and loves us has chosen a special gift, spent money on it, and wrapped it up so that the contents are a surprise.

The giving of a gift is motivated by our affection for another person, who we hope to please. It's exciting to watch them unwrap the gift, eager that it will delight them.

God's great gift to us is Jesus! This gift is not given because we deserve it or have earned it, but it is offered to the world as an expression of His unfathomable love. This gift cost God everything—the very best He had, given to us freely. We cannot pay for it, but we can accept it.

So what is our response to this extraordinary gift from God? It is not right if we receive a present and just store it away without unwrapping it—we need to open it up and discover the contents. Likewise, realizing that Jesus Christ is the very best gift from God is not enough. The receiving part comes first, when we invite Jesus into our hearts to be our Savior and King, but the unwrapping can take a lifetime. We gradually come to understand the richness of who He is and how He wants to be an essential part of our lives.

How do we thank Him for this astonishing gift? As our verse suggests, it is hard to put into words either the wonder of the gift or the Giver. Perhaps, as we learn more about who He is and daily yield our lives to Him, we are saying "thank you" with the love-offering from our hearts.

Whether you need to receive this love gift from Heaven, or begin unwrapping it by developing your relationship with Jesus, be encouraged that God loves you enough to give you the greatest gift of all.

thanks BE TO GOD for HIS inexpressible gift

2 corinthians 9:15

Taking the Passenger Seat

"Trust in the LORD with all your heart, and do not lean on your own understanding"
(Proverbs 3:5, ESV)

The idea of *"leaning on our own under-standing"* brings to mind the leaning tower of Pisa in Italy. Due to soil subsidence, the tower leans quite dramatically to one side and looks as if it might fall over at any moment! **Sometimes, leaning on our own understanding can be just as precarious and unsafe.**

It's natural to rely on what we know and have personally experienced, but this can lead to doing things or facing situations only out of habit. Our perspectives are often so narrow. God, however, has the complete picture, and in Jesus *"are hidden all the treasures of wisdom and knowledge"* (Colossians 2:3). Therefore, looking to Him for solutions and help in times of decision-making is surely the answer.

If we trust the Lord with all our heart, we will be challenged to let go of full control of our lives and to offer Jesus the driver's seat. This means that His hand is on the steering wheel and His foot is on the brakes or accelerator. **Our drive through life is far more exciting and also far safer with Jesus leading and guiding us.** God declares that He

has *"plans to prosper you and not to harm you, plans to give you hope and a future"* (Jeremiah 29:11, NIV).

To move over into the passenger seat of your life may feel rather risky; but, if it is the fullness of God's plan and destiny for your life that you want, then it is also the best and most courageous decision you will ever make.

As you color, allow the Lord to challenge you in the areas of your life that need to be handed over to Him. The Christian life isn't intended to be a boring one! God wants us to live life to the full and to be willing to make a real impact for Him . . . are you ready?

TRUST IN THE LORD WITH ALL YOUR heart DO NOT lean on YOUR own understanding

PROVERBS.3:5
(esv)

In Prayer and Praise

"Bless the LORD, O my soul" (Psalm 103:1, ESV)

DAY 24

Many times in Scripture we are encouraged to "rejoice in the Lord!"

Occasionally, we are guilty of coming to God with a list of the things that we would like Him to do for us. We can be in danger of seeking His hand (what He can offer us) before His face (who He is). It is not wrong to ask the Lord for help, but if this is our primary aim, we may miss out on developing a truly deep and real relationship with Him.

If we focus first on God's magnificence, holiness and supremacy, before taking anything to Him in prayer, it reminds us that He is our powerful Creator, able to help us in all our circumstances. What is more, we are encouraged to come to Him with thankful hearts—*"Enter his gates with thanksgiving and his courts with praise"* (Psalm 100:4, ESV).

It is astonishing that we can, *"with confidence draw near to the throne of grace, that we may receive mercy and find grace to help in time of need"* (Hebrews 4:16, ESV). We have assurance that the King of Kings and Lord of Lords will meet with us and respond to us in love, as He is our wise Father who knows what is best for us.

Do you sometimes wonder why your prayers appear to remain unanswered? Or do you ever feel that God might be ignoring you? Be assured that it is never God's heart to disregard His beloved children, for He is the Alpha and Omega, the Beginning and the End, and He knows your past, your present and will guide you in the future, if you allow Him.

When we are able to approach the Lord with reverence, trust and, even thanksgiving, despite our circumstances, the times of waiting will be a little easier.

Think about some of the amazing attributes of God and spend some time praising Him for who He is.

Bless the LORD O MY SOUL

PSALM 103:1 esv

Being Led by the Good Shepherd

"He leads me beside the still waters. He restores my soul" (Psalm 23:2-3)

The imagery of Psalm 23 paints an incredible picture of what it means to be cared for by Jesus, our Good Shepherd, through all of life's seasons.

The psalm begins with the words *"The Lord is . . ."* He is with us here and now, just as a shepherd is always with his sheep.

Perhaps this picture of a shepherd is unfamiliar in Western cultures. In Middle Eastern countries, a shepherd lives with his sheep and constantly provides for, protects, and guides them. He will sometimes leave the flock to bring back a sheep who has wandered off (Matthew 18:12). By day, he leads them to the best feeding grounds and looks for the sweetest water for them to drink. At night, he keeps watch over them.

Jesus said, *"I am the good shepherd. The good shepherd lays down His life for the sheep"* (John 10:11, ESV). Our Savior promises to defend, protect, lovingly discipline, and care for us. He gives us refreshment if we walk alongside Him, and He knows when we need rest. **His desire is to restore our souls.**

John 10:5 says that, as the Lord's sheep, we will run away from strangers because we do not know their voices. But today's distractions and noise sometimes make it difficult to hear or distinguish the Lord's voice. Many times we hear Christians say wistfully, "God doesn't speak to me." Perhaps they expect to hear audible words? Christians have occasionally experienced this, but more often we will recognize God's "voice" in everyday situations. A passage of Scripture may leap off the page at us, providing challenge, confirmation, or comfort, or the beauty of the natural world may reveal His heart and character (Romans 1:20). Often, our own thoughts are inspired by our Father as He speaks directly to us.

Remember that even in our most desperate times, our Good Shepherd is with us. In dark times, turn your face to the Son, the lover of your soul. He longs to lead you through life's valleys when they come.

Light in the Darkness

"The LORD is my light and my salvation; whom shall I fear? The LORD is the stronghold of my life; of whom shall I be afraid?" (Psalm 27:1, ESV)

Can you imagine living in pitch darkness; a world where no color, texture, or movement can be seen? There would be no sense of space, shape, or perspective. How dreadful! Thankfully, God's first act of creation was to bring light and life into just such an environment, as we read in the very first few sentences of the Bible.

God is still the source of light in our lives today, as beautifully described in Isaiah 60:19: *"The sun shall be no more your light by day, nor for brightness shall the moon give you light; but the LORD will be your everlasting light, and your God will be your glory"* (ESV).

We live in a world where there is a lot of darkness and fear and at points in our lives, even as Christians, we too may experience periods of fear, hopelessness, or depression. How painful it is when we find ourselves in this place. Right in the midst of that despair, allow these words of Jesus to sink deeply into your heart, *"I am the light of the world. Whoever follows me will not walk in darkness, but will have the light of life"* (John 8:12, ESV).

Jesus is indeed our light, our life, and the one who can change our mourning into dancing. That is the truth that we find in Scripture, a solid foundation for our feet and a sure and steadfast hope for our lives.

Be reassured! The Lord is our light and salvation, and we do not need to be afraid.

As you ponder this devotion today, you may want to bring any areas of darkness or despair in your life to Jesus. Listen to Him for His words of love and truth. It may also be helpful to pray through some of these areas with another Christian.

THE LORD IS MY LIGHT AND MY SALVATION

Ps. 27:1

In Christ's Footsteps

"What does the LORD require of you, but to do justly, to love mercy, and to walk humbly with your God?" (Micah 6:8)

This verse can be applied to every area of our lives, and it's such a challenge. How it prompts us to examine our motives and dealings with others!

James 1:22 says that we must not just read or hear the word of God, but do what it says—put it into action. As is often said, actions speak louder than words. What do your actions say about your life and the One you follow?

As we make everyday choices regarding our actions and the path we take in life, do we always act justly, treating everyone with fairness? Justice is one of God's fundamental characteristics (Psalm 89:14, Psalm 33:5), and He desires that it also be the foundation for our decisions. Do you stand for tolerance and respect in your community, seeking justice for those in need?

To *"love mercy"* refers to the heart attitudes that drive our behavior toward others. Jesus says in His Sermon on the Mount, *"Blessed are the merciful, for they shall obtain mercy"* (Matthew 5:7). God's heart is *"merciful and gracious"* (Psalm 103:8). Indeed, it is because of His mercy that we are saved; as

Titus 3:5 puts it: *"not by works of righteousness which we have done, but according to His mercy, He saved us, through the washing of regeneration and renewing of the Holy Spirit."*

To become more Christ-like, we must examine our heart attitudes. Jesus encourages us to be merciful, as our Father in Heaven is merciful. As we build relationships with others, let's remember that mercy triumphs over judgment and that our behavior should demonstrate this (James 2:13). We must seek always to treat others, especially those who are less fortunate than us, with compassion and care.

To *"walk humbly"* with God means giving Him precedence in our lives, and in doing so, valuing and respecting others, instead of being proud or domineering. Humility is best shown by Jesus, so He is surely the perfect example to follow! Walking humbly with God requires us to keep in step with Him, not running ahead or lagging behind.

Do you long to be more Christ-like? Ask Him for grace to enable you to *"love mercy and to walk humbly with your God."*

Sharing God's Love

"Then he said to them, 'Follow me, and I will make you fishers of men'" (Matthew 4:19, ESV)

Jesus called Andrew and his brother Simon Peter to follow Him, leaving life as they knew it behind. As fishermen, they would have appreciated the concept of becoming *"fishers of men."* Later, Jesus likens the Kingdom of Heaven to a *"net that was thrown into the sea and gathered fish of every kind"* (Matthew 13:47, ESV). The different kinds of fish represent people from every tribe and tongue, who were (and are) being called into a new life in Christ.

The call from Jesus to *"make disciples of all nations"* (Matthew 28:19, ESV) is still relevant for us two thousand years later. We are to share the Good News of God's saving grace and love for mankind. In the past, this often meant missionaries spending years living in different countries. Today, sharing the Gospel with all nations can also be done locally in our own communities, as people from many nationalities are spread around the globe. We can rely on the Lord to give us words of hope and encouragement for those who don't yet know Him as Savior and Friend, Lord and Healer.

One day soon Jesus will return for His Church, bringing in a new Heaven and Earth, so there's a great sense of urgency for us to catch fish for the Kingdom of God! Wherever we live and work, we can pray for opportunities to share our faith.

For some, sharing their testimony and starting conversations about the Gospel is easy . . . for others it may be more difficult. We have amazing, often life-changing stories to tell, so take courage! Pray for a holy boldness to share Jesus with those He places on your path.

Group Questions:

1. Take some time to praise God for who He is and all you have learned about His amazing grace.

2. Read Proverbs 3:1–10. Pick out a command to obey, an encouragement, and a challenge, and share them with the group.

3. Do you tend to lean on your own understanding or God's sovereignty in your life? Who is in the driving seat of your life?

4. Micah 6:8 encourages us to do justly, love mercy, and walk humbly with God. How can we do that as we move forward?

Jesus said "FOLLOW me and I will make you fishers of MEN"

matthew 4:19 esv

Notes

More Coloring Books
From Artist Jacqui Grace

Pairing beautiful, hand-drawn illustrations with inspiring Scripture, these full-size books create delightful coloring experiences that renew the mind and refresh the soul.

Images of Grace and
Images of Hope

BETHANYHOUSE

Stay up to date on your favorite books and authors with our free e-newsletters. Sign up today at bethanyhouse.com.

Find us on Facebook. facebook.com/BHPnonfiction

Follow us on Twitter. @bethany_house